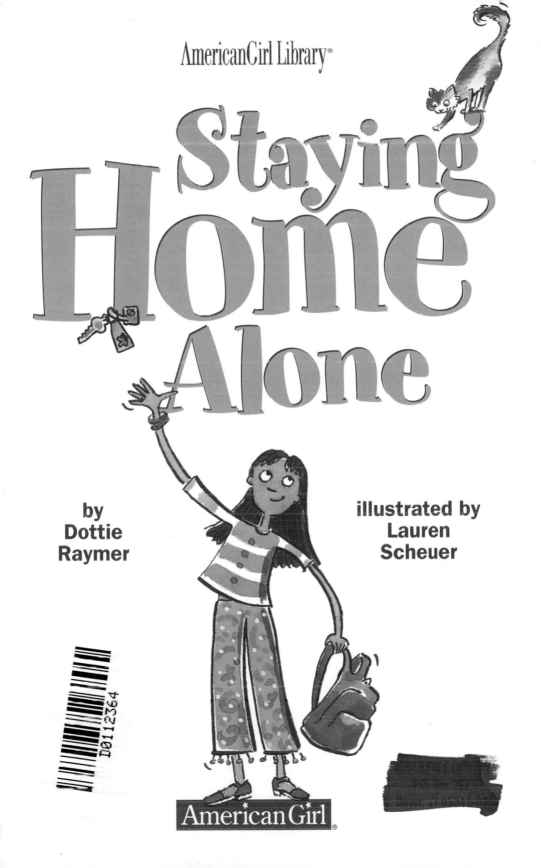

American Girl Library®

Staying Home Alone

by
Dottie
Raymer

illustrated by
Lauren
Scheuer

American Girl®

Published by Pleasant Company
Publications

Copyright © 2002 by Pleasant Company

All rights reserved.
No part of this book may be used
or reproduced in any manner whatsoever
without written permission except in the
case of brief quotations embodied in
critical articles and reviews.

For information, address:
Book Editor
Pleasant Company Publications
8400 Fairway Place
Middleton, WI 53562

Visit our Web site at **americangirl.com**

American Girl® and American Girl Library®
are registered trademarks
of Pleasant Company.

Printed in China
04 05 06 C&C 8 7 6

Editorial Development:
Elizabeth A. Chobanian,
Michelle Watkins

Art Direction and Design:
Chris Lorette David

Book Production:
Kendra Pulvermacher,
Mindy Rappe

A special thanks to:
Molly Kelly,
American Red Cross, Badger Chapter
David A. Riley, Ph.D.
University of Wisconsin–Madison/Extension

Library of Congress
Cataloging-in-Publication Data
Raymer, Dottie.
Staying Home Alone: A girl's guide to
feeling safe and having fun/ by Dottie
Raymer; illustrated by Lauren Scheuer.
p. cm.
2001050093

Summary: Explains what to expect
when one is left home alone and how to
respond when the unexpected happens,
with activities to help learn about one's
home, neighborhood, and capabilities.
ISBN 1-58485-506-1
1. Children's accidents—Prevention—
Juvenile literature. 2. Home accidents—
Prevention—Juvenile literature.
3. Safety education—Juvenile literature.
[1. Accidents. 2. Safety.]
I. Scheuer, Lauren, ill. II. Title.
HV675.72 .R38 2002
613.6—dc21

Dear Reader,

Now that you're getting older, there may be times when you'll be on your own. The house may seem a little quieter. A doorbell might make you jump. And you might not always be sure what to do.

Whether you're ready to stay home alone or just thinking about it, this is your guide to getting prepared. Tips, quizzes, and great advice will help you feel safe and have fun. Be sure to share this book with your parents, so you *all* know what to expect—and what to do when the unexpected happens.

Like anything, feeling comfortable when you're alone takes knowledge and practice. The more you know, the more confident you—and your parents—will be. Together, make a plan and stick to it. That's the real key to feeling in control when you're on your own.

Your friends at American Girl

Contents

Are You Ready? . . . 6

Find out whether you're ready
to stay home alone, and learn what
you need to know before you do.

Be Prepared . . . 16

Get to know your house, your neighborhood,
and the tricks to staying safe.

Coming Home . . . 28

From sibling survival to snack attacks,
here's what to do once you've locked the
door behind you.

Boredom Busters . . . 42

Learn new ways to have fun and make the most of your time alone.

Stay in Control . . . 52

Get tips on first aid plus safety for emergencies and mishaps.

Need-to-Know Info . . . 64

Use these tools to help you— and your family—keep track of need-to-know info.

Are You Ready?

Key thought:

Talk it over.

Get together with your parents. Talk over any questions you have, and find out what's expected of you. The more information you have, the more prepared you'll be.

Ready or Not?

Are you calm in a crisis? Or do sticky situations catch you off guard? How you handle the unexpected will give you an idea of how comfortable you'll feel by yourself. **Take this quiz to find out:**

1. You and your mom are shopping for back-to-school clothes. You turn around to show your mom a shirt, and she's not there! You . . .

   a. decide to keep shopping. She'll catch up with you sooner or later.

   b. stay where you are. It's where she last saw you, so it'll be the first place she'll look when she discovers you've been separated.

   c. run through the store shouting, "Mom! Mom! Where are you?"

2. Your big science report is due today, and you just realized you left it on your desk at home. You . . .

   a. say, "Oh, well, I wasn't doing that great in science anyway."

   b. tell your teacher what happened and ask her to help you figure out what to do.

   c. call your dad and ask him to go home and get the report for you.

3. You wake up in the middle of the night and see a strange shadow in the corner of your room. You . . .

   a. tell yourself it's just your imagination, and go back to sleep.

   b. turn on the light to make sure it really is just your bathrobe on the back of a chair.

   c. call out to your parents.

4. Everybody's been talking about the new giant slide at Water World. But nobody told you it was *this* giant! You . . .

   a. shout, "Let's go for it!" and race to the top.

   b. say to a friend, "I'll try it if you will."

   c. tell your friends, "I'll wait here. You go ahead."

5. Your aunt gives you a new camera for your birthday. But you need to learn how to use it before you snap any pictures. You . . .

   a. toss aside the directions and figure out how to load the film yourself.

   b. dive into the directions. If you have any questions, you'll ask your mom.

   c. give the directions to your mom. Once she's read them, she can teach you.

6. Your dad is 15 minutes late picking you up from soccer practice. You . . .

   a. walk to the nearest store and buy a can of soda. At least you won't die of thirst while you wait.

   b. stay at your pickup point and dig a book out of your backpack to pass the time.

   c. worry that he forgot to pick you up and ask a friend's mom for a ride.

7. You're washing your hands in the bathroom at school when the fire alarm goes off. You . . .

   a. finish washing your hands. It's probably just a drill.

   b. go back to your classroom immediately—dripping hands and all.

   c. run out of the building in a panic.

Answers

Daring Daisy

You've probably been feeling ready to stay home alone for a while now. You're easygoing and feel sure you can handle any challenge that comes your way. But sometimes you may be too quick to respond. Slow down. Take some time to think before you act. Thinking things through will help you make good decisions on your own.

Mostly **b**'s

Reliable Rose

You are capable and reliable—two great qualities! You're probably ready to stay home by yourself, but you may still be feeling a little uncertain. Perhaps you're worried that you'll have too much responsibility, or that you'll get lonely or bored. Talk with your parents about what is worrying you. Together, you can figure out what you need to feel comfortable with the new arrangement.

Mostly C's

Panicky Petunia

You may like the idea of staying home alone, but it doesn't take much to give you the jitters. Why not try a couple of test runs first—say, while your mom or dad goes on an errand or to visit with a neighbor. If you still don't feel ready, tell your parents how you feel and ask them to help you find an alternative. Your school counselor can tell you about other options that are available in your area.

House Rules

Different families have different rules. Talk with your parents about your family's house rules. That way, you'll both know what to expect about what you can—and can't—do when you're home alone.

Check In

You get home, lock the door behind you, and then what? You probably need to check in with an adult. Ask your parents who you should check in with and how.

Hel-lo?

What do you do when the phone rings? Do you answer it? Let the answering machine pick it up? If you do answer it, what do you say? Is there a time limit on calls to friends?

Ding-Dong!

The best house rule is not to answer the door at all. If you have a short list of people you can allow in when you're alone, come up with a system so you know who's at the door before you open it.

Net-Wise

Are you allowed to e-mail friends? Check certain Web sites? Enter chatrooms? Surf the Internet? Find out how your parents feel about you logging on when you're home alone.

Home Turf

For some girls, "home" means "in the house." For others, it means "in the yard" or "in the neighborhood." Ask your parents what your home territory is.

Snack Time

What are you allowed to snack on when you get home? Can you make it yourself? Are there any foods or appliances that are off-limits?

On Schedule

Do homework . . . or play with the cat? Shoot baskets . . . or clean your room? Your parents might have one opinion. You might have another. Talk about it, and work out a schedule that suits you both.

Golden Rules

Even though every family has different rules, there are some basic rules that apply to everyone. Follow these golden rules, and you'll feel—and be—in control!

. . . always lock the door.

Believe it or not, leaving your key in the door is an easy thing to do. Avoid this mistake by forming a good habit. As soon as you walk in the door, put your key in a special spot, like a hook or a dish. Make it the first thing you do when you shut the door behind you.

. . . check in.

Always let your parents know where you are. Call to keep your parents up-to-date if your schedule changes from week to week. And always check with a parent before you change your plans.

. . . never tell anyone I'm alone.

You can be polite without letting people know you're alone. If someone calls for your mom, simply say, "My mom's busy right now. May I take a message?" If the caller is persistent, ignore any questions. Say, "I'll let her know you called," and hang up.

Mew

... trust my instincts.

If you're feeling uncomfortable about a situation, pay attention to that gut feeling. Your instincts help keep you alert, and if something doesn't feel right—the walk home, a neighbor, anything—call your parents. It's never silly to listen to those "funny feelings."

... never let anyone in the house.

Your best bet is to never unlock the door and never let anyone in the house. Ignoring the doorbell isn't rude if it keeps you safe. Talk to your parents about specific rules for your house.

I promise to ...

... have a back-up plan.

No matter how prepared you are, accidents happen. Whether you've lost your key, missed the bus, or forgotten your homework at school, you need to have a back-up plan when something goes wrong. Talk to your parents about what to do—and who to turn to for help—when things don't go according to plan.

Be Prepared

Key thought:

Know where things are.

Whether it's your house key or a pay phone, knowing where something is at the time you need it will keep you safe and in control.

Pocket Power

Before you leave your house, make sure you have what you need to get home safely. Keep these VIPs—Very Important Possessions—tucked safely inside a pocket in your backpack.

Emergency Snack

You can't think straight when you're hungry. An extra granola bar will keep away those hunger pangs until you get home.

Emergency Numbers

Keep your parents' work numbers and other emergency numbers handy on a wallet-sized card.

House Key

Don't hang it on your belt or backpack strap for anyone to see. Hide it away, safe and sound.

Phone or Bus Change

Be sure that you have the exact change you would need.

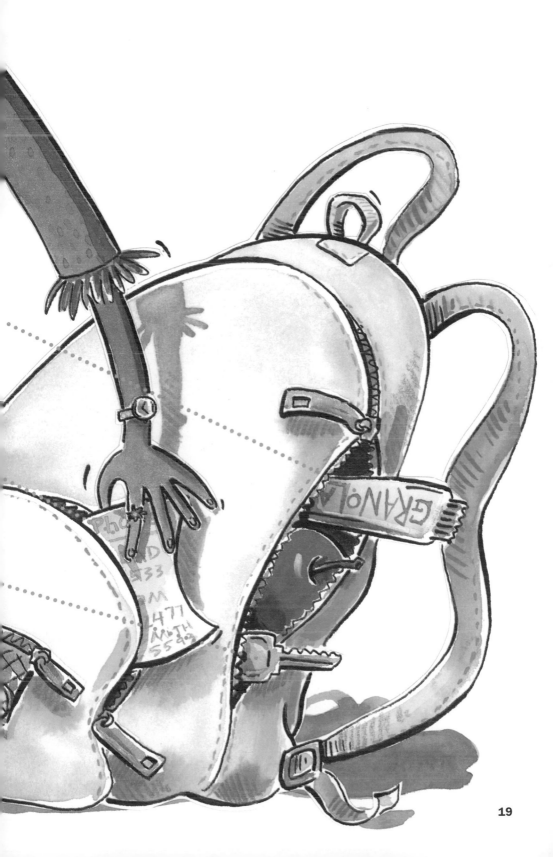

Your Neighborhood

Chances are, you're pretty familiar with your neighborhood. But **think about it:** do you know the safe places you can go—and the not-so-safe places you need to avoid? Here are some things to look for the next time you take a walk around the block:

Public places. Small neighborhood businesses or community centers are good places to go when you're in a jam.

Street names. Know the nearest cross street to your house. If you call an emergency number, the operator might ask you for this information.

Creepy spots. Steer clear of places, such as alleys or empty buildings, that make you feel uncomfortable.

MAIN

Pay phone. If you're locked out, knowing where to make a call means you're one step closer to getting help.

APPLE LANE

HoMe

Friendly neighbor #1. Is there a trusted neighbor home during the day? If so, talk to your mom about giving her a spare house key.

GRoVe

Friendly neighbor #2. Have a back-up person to turn to for help, just in case the person you would usually go to isn't home.

Key Care

Where would you be without your house key? Locked out, that's where! Take good care of your key, and it'll take care of you.

- **DO** keep your key out of sight. If you wear your key around your neck, keep it tucked inside your shirt. If you want to keep it on a key chain, attach the chain to a loop inside your backpack or hide it in a zippered pocket.

- **DO** make sure you remove your key from the door when you get inside the house. Then lock the door behind you.

- **DO** make sure that a trusted neighbor has an extra key. No matter how careful you are, the day may come when you forget or lose your key. If that happens, go directly to your neighbor. Then call your parents and let them know what happened.

- **DON'T** hide an extra key outside your house. Police say that burglars know all the good hiding places, too!

- **DON'T** lend your key to anyone—not even a friend.

- **DON'T** write your name or address on the key. You don't want to give a stranger a written invitation to your house!

Got It?

A good set of supplies will help you feel confident and in control! Make sure you know where everything on this list is kept.

Family Calendar

Hang a large calendar on the wall. Get into the habit of jotting your schedule on the calendar. Get others in your family into the same habit, so you know where they will be, too.

First-Aid Kit

You can buy a complete kit at a pharmacy. Or you and your parents can make your own. Call the Red Cross or a local hospital to find out what items to include in the kit.

Emergency Phone Number List

Use the list in the back of this book to keep track of your parents' work numbers, the numbers of the police and fire departments, and other important telephone numbers.

Flashlight with Extra Batteries

Don't use candles and matches. They are unreliable and a fire hazard.

Message Board

A dry-erase board or a bulletin board will keep your family's lines of communication open. If the board is next to the telephone, so much the better! If not, make sure there is a notepad handy for phone messages.

MeM

dad,
Aunt Rose
called.

Soccer ga
tuesday

Emergency Fund

Keep $20 in cash, and change for a pay phone, in a safe place. And remember— no borrowing from the emergency fund for ice cream!

Battery-Operated Radio

This radio is for emergencies, not for listening to your favorite tunes! If your electricity goes out in a storm, it will come in handy for weather bulletins.

Home Sweet Home

You want to feel comfortable when you're home by yourself—and you can. That comfort starts with knowing your house is as safe as can be. See how many things on this list you can find:

- Deadbolt locks

- Smoke detectors (at least one on each floor)

- Outside lights

- Peephole in front door

- List of emergency numbers by phone

- Closed windows with locks

- First-aid kit on shelf in bathroom

- Flashlights on shelf in kitchen

* Is your house missing anything on the list? If so, talk to a parent about it.
The more things you can check off, the more prepared you'll be.

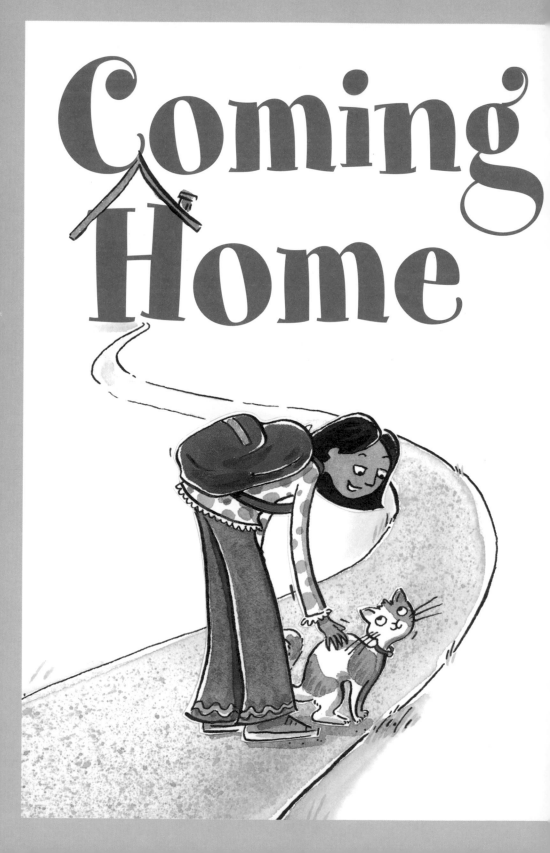

Coming Home

Key thought:

Use your head.

Making good choices starts with using your own best judgment. Take the time to think things through, and you won't go wrong.

It's Your Choice

When you walk in the door, you have lots of choices to make. See if you make the right ones by finding your way through this maze.

Key crisis! If you don't return your key to the same spot every day, you'll probably end up losing it. Start over at the front door.

I make a call . . .
to check in with Mom.
to talk with a friend.

My coat goes . . .
in the closet.
on the floor.

I put my key . . . .
near my backpack.
on its hook.

START

Messed up! It's easy to toss your coat on the floor. But if you put things away to begin with, you won't have to clean up after yourself. Start over at the front door.

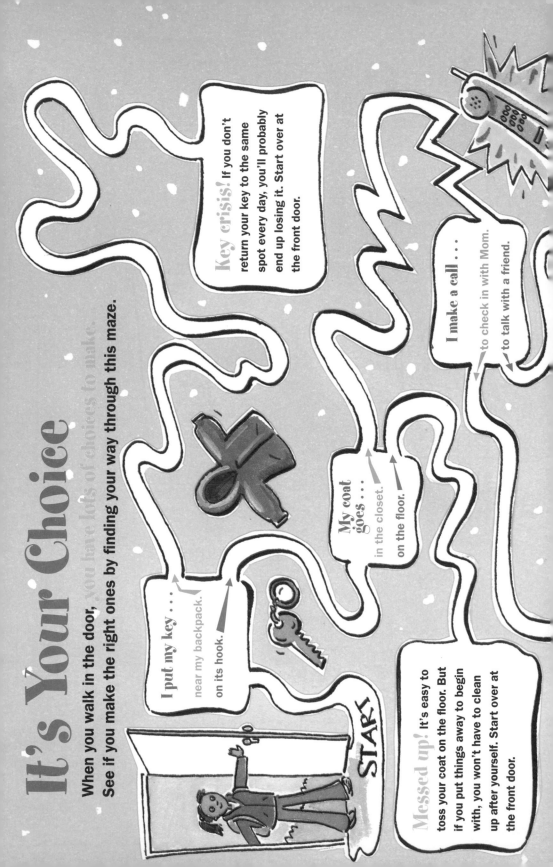

I'm Not Scared . . .

Everybody feels scared at times. It's your body's way of keeping you alert and ready to take action. Tell a parent or other adult how you feel. **They can help you** take control of your fear.

Where's My Mom?

Your mom is usually home by 5:30. But it's 6:00, and she's not home yet. You know she's probably still at work, **but you can't help worrying.**

Time passes quickly for your mom as she's rushing to leave work. But those extra minutes may seem like an eternity to you as you wait for her return. Tell her how you feel. Work out a system for letting you know when she's going to be late. Make sure you and she agree on what "late" means—five minutes after she's expected, fifteen minutes, half an hour? Know who to call when your mom is late and can't be reached.

. . . Am I?

It's Too Dark!

You hate October. That's when the days start getting shorter. And coming home to **a dark, empty house gives you the creeps!**

Tell your parents how you feel. They can install a light timer so that one or two lights will be on when you get home from school. They can also ask a neighbor to turn on an outside light when it begins to get dark. After you lock the door behind you, turn on all the lights you need to feel comfortable, and close the curtains. And if there's a room in your house that feels particularly dark, put an extra light there, too.

What's That Noise?

You're doing your homework when you hear the floor creak downstairs. Your heart begins to thump. **Is there somebody there?** Or is it just your imagination?

Tame noises that make you nervous by getting to know them. Go on a noise hunt with an adult. Make a list of the sounds and ask the adult to help you find an explanation for each noise. Maybe it's a tree branch hitting a window, or the air vents creaking. If the noises still bother you, try turning on the radio or television to drown them out.

Sibling Struggles

Brothers and sisters. Sometimes they're your best friends, and other times you'd rather be alone. It's not always easy to get along. But the key to good relationships is good communication. Talking things over with your siblings and your parents can help.

Who's in Charge?

Your mom says you're supposed to look after your **little sister** when you're home by yourselves. But your little sister **won't listen** to a thing you say! Every time you tell her to do something, she says, "You can't make me! You're not my mother!"

Your mom needs to make it clear to your sister that you are in charge. Sit down with your mom and sister and talk about what your responsibilities really are. If you think your mom is expecting too much of you, let her know. If your sister thinks you have too much power, she can let your mom know that, too. Together, you should be able to figure out a balance that works for both you and your sister.

Stuck Indoors

You and your brother are allowed to go to the park, but only if you go together. But **your brother never wants to do anything** except play games on the computer. You don't think it's fair that you have to stay inside just because your brother won't budge.

Try making a deal with your brother. Maybe he will agree to half an hour of time outdoors if you'll take over a chore. And once you do coax him outside, who knows? He may have so much fun, he'll want to stay longer! If he still won't budge, talk the problem over with your parents. Together, you might be able to come up with some alternatives. Your parents may decide that they want your brother to spend more time outdoors, too. Or they may give you permission to go to the park with a friend.

Tattle Trouble

Your brother has a really bad temper. Whenever you don't do what he wants, he punches you or knocks you down. If you threaten to tell, he calls you a tattletale and a baby. You don't want to be a tattletale, but **sometimes it hurts!**

Here's a rule to go by: If anyone—no matter who it is—is hurting you, it's time to tell. It's not tattling. It's protecting yourself. Find a time when you can talk to a parent in private. If that doesn't help, find another adult you can trust. Your brother is being a bully, and he needs to be stopped.

Boredom Bickering

Your dad says that you and your sisters squabble because you can't find anything better to do. Well, he's right. **There isn't anything better to do!**

A little imagination can go a long way when you're hanging around with nothing to do. Put together a talent show for the other members of your family. If you're tired of Sorry! or Monopoly, create a new board game based on a book or movie you all like. Plan a special family feast—right down to the shopping list. Get a book of card games from the library, and challenge yourselves to learn one new game a week. Don't forget the Fun-for-One activities on page 48 of this book. What's fun for one is usually even more fun with two or three!

Sibling-Saver Gadgets

Got sibling struggles? One of these relationship-saving devices can help:

▪ Headphones
Your sister can't think without her favorite music, but you need complete silence to study. A set of headphones for your sister will solve this problem.

▪ Kitchen Timer
Is one of you a phone or computer hog? Set a timer! When the buzzer sounds, it's time to get off.

▪ Memo Pad
Got a gripe? Write it down on a pad of paper. If it's still important at the end of the day, give the memo to your mom or dad and find a quiet time to discuss the situation.

I'm Starving!

Got an attack of the munchies? Grab a snack that's tasty and good for you, too! You don't need to use appliances to whip up something delicious. Here are some no-bake, simple ideas:

EZ Pizzas

These fresh pizzas need no baking. Spread cream cheese carefully onto a graham cracker. Decorate it with fresh fruit. Or try vegetable slices on wheat crackers.

Crunchy Munchies

Make your own trail mix. Combine handfuls of snacks—nuts, cereal, dried fruit, mini crackers, pretzels, and a few chocolate chips—in one bowl. Mix it up and munch away.

PB Dip

In a container, stir together $1/4$ cup peanut butter and $1/4$ cup strawberry yogurt. Use mixture as a dip for pretzels, pita slices, fruit, and veggies.

Veggie Sandwich

Make a salad sandwich. Spread veggie cream cheese on bread. Layer with cucumber slices, tomatoes, and lettuce.

Deli Roll

Start with a Romaine lettuce leaf. On top of it, layer a slice of lunch meat and a slice of cheese. Roll and eat!

Fancy Fruit

Stick bamboo skewers through strawberries, grapes, and apple slices. Spoon yogurt into a small dish and use it as a dipping sauce.

Kitchen Basics

1. Follow the house rules for using appliances, knives, and other kitchen tools.

2. Wash your hands with soap and water before handling food.

3. Wipe up all spills as soon as they happen.

4. Put away food, rinse or wash all dishes, and wipe off the counter after you are finished.

Sweet Treats

Satisfy a sweet tooth with one of these fruity treats.

Berry Delight

- Angel food cake
- Strawberries
- Whipped topping

Cut a slice of angel food cake into cubes. Layer strawberry slices, cake cubes, and whipped topping in a dish. End with a dollop of whipped topping and a few strawberries.

Yogurt Pop

- Any flavor yogurt
- Plastic spoon

Open a small yogurt container, stick in a plastic spoon, and freeze overnight. The next day, dip the container in warm water, twist the spoon, slide the container off, and you've got a tasty yogurt pop.

Fruity Parfait

- Plain or vanilla yogurt
- Blueberries, raspberries, or strawberries
- Rice Krispies or granola

Layer plain or vanilla yogurt, blueberries, raspberries, or strawberries, and Rice Krispies or granola. Top it all off with another scoop of yogurt.

Scoop O' Fruit

- Cantaloupe, watermelon, or honeydew melon
- Yogurt
- Cereal
- Strawberry

Use an ice cream scoop to scrape out long, thin strips of melon. The strips will curl into balls like ice cream. Top with your favorite yogurt, some dry cereal, and a strawberry.

Pineapple Fizz

- Pineapple juice concentrate
- Lemon-lime soda

In a pitcher, mix 1 can of pineapple juice concentrate (pourable or frozen) and 3 cans of lemon-lime soda. Stir gently.

Cookies 'n' Cream

- Cream cheese
- Orange juice concentrate
- Ricotta cheese
- Butter cookies
- Vanilla pudding
- Raspberries
- Whipped topping

In a large bowl, combine 3 ounces softened cream cheese, 1 cup ricotta cheese, 1 cup prepared vanilla pudding, and 1/3 cup thawed orange juice concentrate. Mix well with a fork or whisk. Crumble butter cookies and layer with cream cheese mixture. Add whipped topping, raspberries, and a cookie on top.

Boredom Busters

Key thought:

Have fun!

Being alone doesn't have to be boring. Grab a good book. Practice the piano. Make the most of your time, and it will fly by quickly.

It's About Time

How do you handle your time? Are you the early bird that gets the worm? Or do you believe that haste makes waste? Pick the answers that describe you best.

1. The first thing you do when you get home from school is . . .

   a. flop on your bed and stare at the ceiling.

   b. make a snack and look through the mail.

   c. start in on your homework to get it out of the way.

2. You have a big project due on Thursday. It's Monday. You . . .

   a. make a mental note to think about the project on Wednesday.

   b. make a list of things you need to do to get the project done.

   c. already feel behind on your research.

3. You're supposed to practice your trumpet 30 minutes every day. You . . .

   a. plan to practice an hour every other day instead—starting tomorrow.

   b. set a timer for 30 minutes at the beginning of your practice session.

   c. squeeze the 30 minutes in between soccer practice and Girl Scouts.

4. You and a friend are working on a class project together. You . . .

   a. tell her not to worry. You'll get your part of the project done—eventually.

   b. set up some times when you can get together and work on the project.

   c. finish your part of the project right away so that you can help her with her part.

5. You don't have enough time to finish your homework before dinner, so you . . .

   a. watch TV instead.

   b. start an assignment anyway so there will be less to do after dinner.

   c. ask your mom if you can eat while you work.

6. If you could change the time you go to school, it would be . . .

   a. later, so you could sleep longer in the morning.

   b. about the same.

   c. earlier, so you could fit more activities into your day.

Answers

Behind Time

You like to take things slow and easy. People like being around you—you seem to have a knack for calming things down. Unfortunately, the rest of the world doesn't always work at your easygoing pace. You also may have a tendency to procrastinate, which means that things like chores and schoolwork don't always get done on time.

Timely Tip: Try hanging a fun wall calendar in a place where you can't miss it. Jot down important activities and due dates. Then take a minute to check the calendar each day so you don't get yourself into a bind.

Mostly **b**'s

On Time

You're usually on time, but you don't make a big deal of it. You like to keep an even pace, and plan ahead when you need to. Your friends appreciate your common sense and know that they can count on you to get the job done.

Timely Tip: Got something super important to remember? Pin a reminder on your backpack. A favorite button or ribbon will catch your eye. Use the same thing every time, and it'll jog your memory whenever you see it.

Mostly **C**'s

Ahead of Time

You are reliable and well organized and have a reputation for getting things done on time. You like to know what to expect and feel best when you have everything under control. Your friends sometimes call you a worrywart, but they admire how you stay on top of things.

Timely Tip: Make sure you don't leave having fun out of your busy schedule! At the beginning of the week, go over your calendar and find time each day that you can set aside for "doing nothing." Mark that spot with a sticker as a reminder that it's time to relax and have fun!

Fun-for-One!

Being alone means no interruptions and no distractions. So if you like to do something that requires privacy or total concentration, now's your time to do it.

Top Ten Things to Do When You're Home Alone

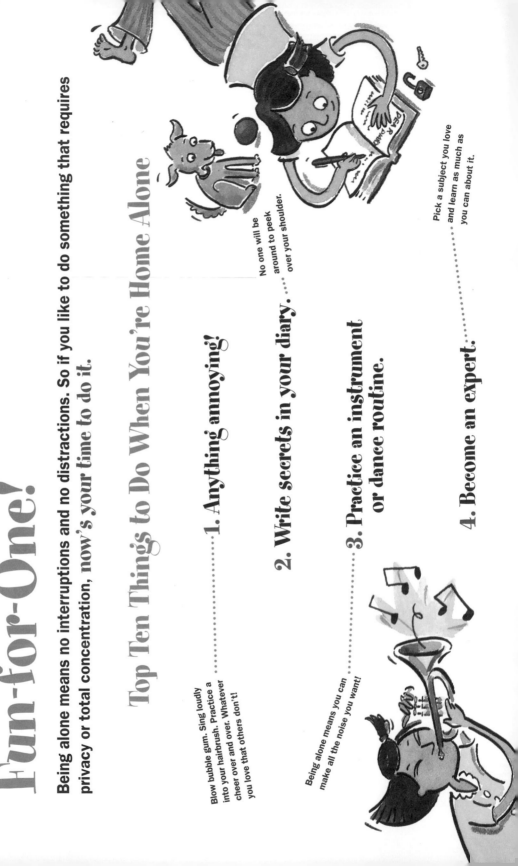

1. Anything annoying!

Blow bubble gum. Sing loudly into your hairbrush. Practice a cheer over and over. Whatever you love that others don't!

Being alone means you can make all the noise you want!

2. Write secrets in your diary.

No one will be around to peek over your shoulder.

3. Practice an instrument or dance routine.

4. Become an expert.

Pick a subject you love and learn as much as you can about it.

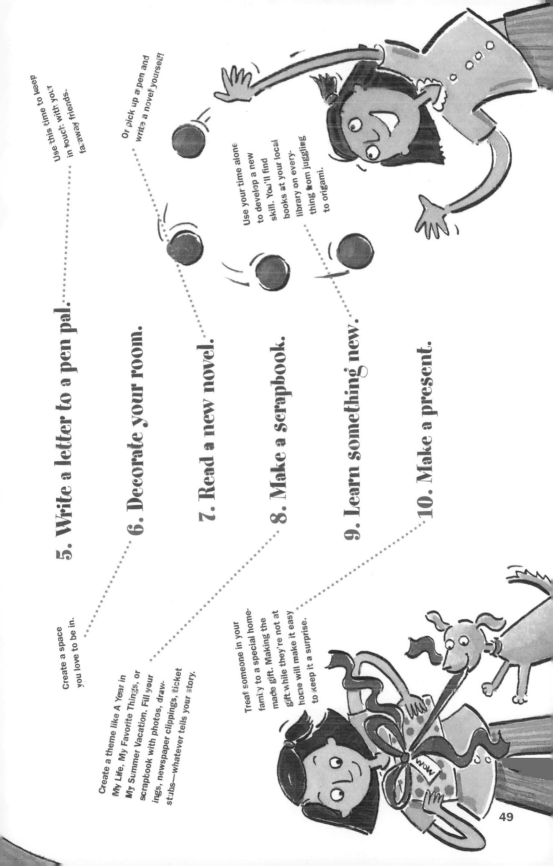

5. Write a letter to a pen pal.

Use this time to keep in touch with your far-away friends.

6. Decorate your room.

Create a space you love to be in.

7. Read a new novel.

Or pick up a pen and write a novel yourself!

8. Make a scrapbook.

Create a theme like A Year in My Life, My Favorite Things, or My Summer Vacation. Fill your scrapbook with photos, drawings, newspaper clippings, ticket stubs—whatever tells your story.

9. Learn something new.

Use your time alone to develop a new skill. You'll find books at your local library on everything from juggling to origami.

10. Make a present.

Treat someone in your family to a special home-made gift. Making the gift while they're not at home will make it easy to keep it a surprise.

Keep in Touch

"Alone" doesn't have to mean "lonely." Here are some ways to connect with family and friends, even when they aren't around.

Keep a conversation journal.

Is there something you're just dying to tell your dad (or somebody else)? Jot it down in a journal or little notebook. Slip it in his briefcase along with a note asking for a response. Keep passing the notebook back and forth. You can carry on an entire conversation without speaking a word!

Start a virtual book club.

Make a plan with a friend or family member to read the same book at the same time. Decide how much of the book you will read at one time. Then arrange a phone call to talk about what you've read.

Pass notes.

Keep a daily journal with your friends. Fill it with doodles, thoughts, fortunes, fill-in-the-blank questions, and the latest news at school. Assign a day of the week to each friend. When it's your turn to take it home, you can respond to what the last person wrote. It's like passing notes in class—only you're writing at home, so you won't get in trouble! Don't forget to surprise the next person in line with a special treat— tuck in stickers, a coupon, or a special cartoon to make her smile.

Send a friend a smile.

Whether your friend lives across the country or across the street, brighten her day with a handwritten letter or homemade card. Get creative by including drawings, puzzles, and fill-in-the-blank questions.

Key thought:

Trust your instincts.

If something doesn't feel quite right, don't ignore that gut feeling. Your instincts are like a little voice reminding you to be careful.

Tricky Situations

What do you do when you're not sure what to do? Trust your instincts!

Can't Wait to Chat

Your friend just gave you the Internet address for a cool new chatroom. Your mom and dad have said that **they want to O.K. any chatrooms** you want to enter. By the time they get home from work, though, there won't be any time left to chat!

Save your chatter for one more day. If the chatroom is as cool as your friend says it is, it'll still be there tomorrow—after your parents have had a chance to check it out. Internet chatrooms are a great way to meet people online. The problem is that you can't know for sure exactly who it is you're meeting. Your parents—and you—are right to be cautious.

Funny Feelings

You're practicing cartwheels in your front yard, when you notice **an unfamiliar van parked across the street.** The driver is sitting behind the wheel, smoking a cigarette. Come to think of it, the same van was parked in the same place yesterday.

There's no law against sitting in a parked car. Maybe the driver is just taking a break, but it's not up to you to figure that out. Something about that van is making you nervous. **Follow that instinct.** Go inside and lock the door behind you. Tell your parents about the van (or point it out if it's still there when they get home).

Wow! Was that a tough soccer practice! Luckily, there's a park bench at your bus stop. You plop down, glad to be off your feet. After a few minutes, a woman comes along and sits down next to you. Although she seems friendly at first, you feel she's asking you too many questions about yourself. You begin to get **a funny feeling in your stomach.**

Listen to your body. That funny feeling is telling you something. The woman might be perfectly harmless, but she is too close for comfort. **Move away,** even if it means having to get up on those tired feet. It's always a good idea to keep at least two arm lengths between you and any stranger. If you start feeling even more uncomfortable, go to a safe place and phone a parent or other adult you trust. It's worth missing the bus to play it safe.

Hold the Phone!

A woman on the telephone says she works with your dad. She wants to drop off some important papers for him to sign, but she forgot to get the address from him. **If you'll give her your address,** she'll bring the papers right by.

Something here doesn't make sense. If she works with your dad, why can't she get your address from his workplace, or better yet, leave the papers there? You know not to give out information over the telephone anyway. Tell the woman you'll have your mom or dad call her back.

The phone rings, but when you say "Hello," nobody answers. You're pretty sure it's a group of boys from your class making prank calls. They may be having fun, but you're not. **And the calls are getting annoying.**

Even if you think the pranksters are kids you know, **don't play along** with their game. When the phone rings, don't answer it. If you have an answering machine, let it pick up the message. Chances are, the pranksters will get bored with their little game, and quit calling. Let your parents know what's going on and that you won't be answering the phone. If the phone calls continue, talk over possible solutions to the problem with your parents.

Who's There?

You're sitting at the dining room table doing your homework when **you notice someone pass by** outside. You sneak up to the window to get a better look, and you see a man next to the house!

Don't panic. During the day, a variety of service people can show up at your house—from a cable repairperson to the utility meter reader. Most of the time, their work is done outside your house, and they won't come to your door. So stay put, take a breath, and **call your mom** to let her know what's going on. If someone should ring the doorbell, it's best not to answer it. Whoever it is can come back another time or leave a note for your parents. Let your mom and dad know someone was there, and they can look into it.

What Do You DO?

Do you know what to do in an emergency? Babysitters' training courses like the ones offered by the American Red Cross will teach you the basics. Some organizations like hospitals and YMCAs offer classes just for kids who stay home alone. These tips will also help you stay in control:

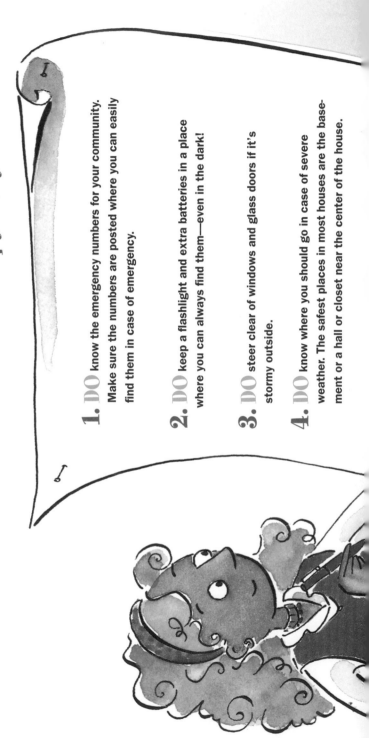

1. **DO** know the emergency numbers for your community. Make sure the numbers are posted where you can easily find them in case of emergency.

2. **DO** keep a flashlight and extra batteries in a place where you can always find them—even in the dark!

3. **DO** steer clear of windows and glass doors if it's stormy outside.

4. **DO** know where you should go in case of severe weather. The safest places in most houses are the basement or a hall or closet near the center of the house.

5. **DO** use a battery-operated radio to monitor storm conditions in very bad weather.

6. **DO** leave the house and call 911 from a neighbor's house if you smell gas. It's a funny smell you may not be used to. Your parents can help you recognize it.

7. **DO** keep electrical appliances away from water.

8. **DO** remember the most important thing to do in case of fire: Get out of the house. Go over escape routes with your parents.

9. **DO** make like a snake, and crawl along the floor if you are in a room filled with smoke.

10. **DO** stop, drop, and roll if any part of your clothing catches fire.

Ouch!

Need a Band-Aid . . . or more? Here's what to do:

When you're on your own, you need to rely on your first-aid know-how. The best way to get that information is by attending a first-aid or babysitting class offered by your local hospital or the American Red Cross. When in doubt, call 911 or your local emergency number. For smaller things, like a scrape or a nosebleed, you can use these guidelines:

Choking

- Make a fist.
- Place the thumb side against your belly, just above your belly button.
- Grab the fist with your other hand.
- Thrust or quickly pull your fist up and into your belly.
- Repeat until whatever you're choking on pops out of your mouth.
- Call 911 and then your parents.

Sprained or Twisted Ankle

- Apply ice to your ankle.
- Lie down to rest.
- Keep your ankle raised on the arm of a chair or a pillow, so that your ankle is higher than the rest of your body.

Fever

- If you think you have a fever, let a parent know.
- Drink cool, clear liquids (water or juice).
- DON'T take Tylenol, aspirin, or any other medicine without first getting permission from a parent.

Cuts and Scrapes

- Press a clean cloth or paper towel on the cut to stop the bleeding.
- Wash the cut with soap and water.
- Cover with a Band-Aid.
- Call your parent or 911.

Poisoning

- If you mistakenly swallow anything that isn't food, call the poison control center or 911 immediately.
- Tell the poison control operator what you swallowed, and follow his or her directions carefully.
- DON'T take any medicine unless the poison control operator tells you to.

Nosebleeds

- Sit down, and lean your head forward.
- Pinch the soft part of your nose closed until it stops bleeding.
- If your nose is still bleeding, try pinching it again. If that doesn't help, call your parent or 911.

Bee or Wasp Stings

- Scrape the stinger off with your fingernail, a card, or another stiff item.
- Wash the sting with soap and water.
- Press ice or a cold compress on the area to reduce the pain and swelling.

Burns

- For all burns, immediately place the red area under cold—not icy—running water for at least five minutes.
- If the burn is large, white, or blistering, call 911.
- Don't put anything on the burn—not even a Band-Aid.
- If the burn is still bothering you, call a parent.

Key thought:

Relax–you're in control.

You know what it takes to be coolheaded and confident when you're home alone. Why? You have someone you can really count on—YOU!

Need-to-Know Info

Have the right information at the moment you need it. Here are some ways to **keep track of important info.** Fill in the blanks, tear out the pages, and put them in a place where everyone in your family can use them.

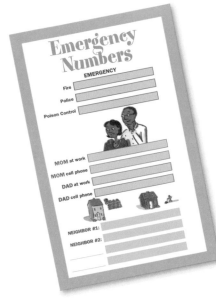

Emergency Numbers List

Keep this list by your telephone. If you have more than one phone in your house, make a copy to keep by each phone.

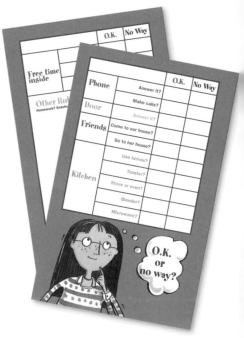

O.K. or No Way?

What's O.K. in your house? What's not O.K.? Ask your mom or dad to help you fill out this list so everyone knows the rules.

Info-to-Go

Fill out a card and stick it in your backpack so you always have important numbers at your fingertips. Don't forget to pop one in your soccer bag or wallet, too!

Emergency Numbers

EMERGENCY

Fire

Police

Poison Control

MOM at work

MOM cell phone

DAD at work

DAD cell phone

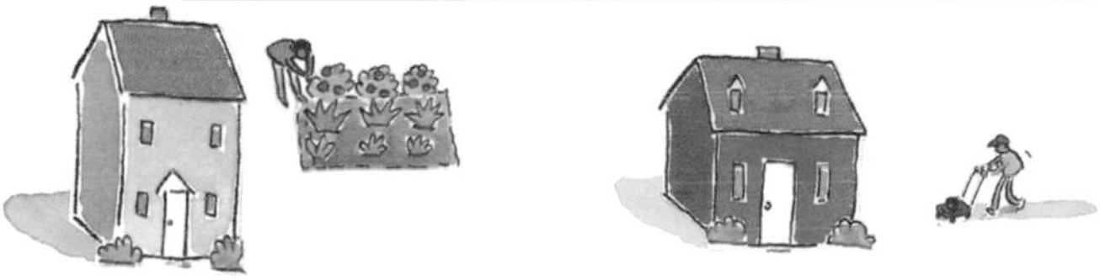

NEIGHBOR #1:

NEIGHBOR #2:

....

....

Emergency Information

An emergency operator will need to know . . .

your name:

your address:

apartment number:

intersecting street or landmark:

your telephone number:

**DON'T HANG UP!
THE OPERATOR WILL
TELL YOU WHAT TO DO!**

		O.K.	No Way
Phone	**Answer it?**		
	Make calls?		
Door	**Answer it?**		
Friends	**Come to our house?**		
	Go to her house?		
Kitchen	**Use knives?**		
	Toaster?		
	Stove or oven?		
	Blender?		
	Microwave?		

O.K.
or
no way?